CW01021641

Seven words from Calvary

A devotional exposition of Christ's words on the cross

Timothy Cross

DayOne

Endorsements

All who open this book are entering a master class as Timothy opens out the words of the Lord Jesus at Calvary. May it bless you through its clear, concise and thought-provoking presentation as much as it has blessed me!

Rev. Ron Keen, Railway Mission chaplain in Wales

A valuable study of these sayings of our Lord Jesus Christ that commends Him as Saviour and encourages believers to understand and value their salvation more fully.

Rev. W. John Cook B.A., B.D., former lecturer in New Testament studies and currently minister of Barry Evangelical Presbyterian Church, South Wales

© Day One Publications 2015
First Edition 2015

All Scripture quotations, unless stated otherwise, are from the Revised Standard Version.

British Library Cataloguing in Publication Data available

ISBN 978-1-84625-452-9

Published by Day One Publications
Ryelands Road, Leominster, HR6 8NZ

☎ 01568 613 740
FAX: 01568 611 473
email—sales@dayone.co.uk
web site—www.dayone.co.uk

All rights reserved

No part of this publication may be reproduced, or stored in a retrieval system, or transmitted, in any form or by any means, mechanical, electronic, photocopying, recording or otherwise, without the prior permission of Day One Publications.

Designed by Rob Jones, Elk Design and printed by TJ International

In loving memory of my father,
John E. Cross

Contents

Preface

It was said of the Lord Jesus Christ that 'No man ever spoke like this man!' (John 7:46). Jesus' first recorded words were 'Did you not know that I must be in my Father's house?' (Luke 2:49). These were spoken in the temple at Jerusalem when He was just twelve years old. They reveal that He was aware of His unique, divine Sonship even at that early age. Jesus' last recorded words, however, were spoken as He suffered and died to redeem sinners on the cross of Calvary. There were seven of these sayings:

- 'Father, forgive them ...' (Luke 23:34).
- 'Truly, I say to you, today you will be with me in Paradise' (Luke 23:43).
- 'Woman, behold, your son! ... Behold, your mother!' (John 19:26–27).
- 'My God, my God, why hast thou forsaken me?' (Matt. 27:46).
- 'I thirst' (John 19:28).
- 'It is finished' (John 19:30).
- 'Father, into thy hands I commit my spirit!' (Luke 23:46).

If the last words of anyone are especially poignant and solemn, how much more so are the last words of the Lord Jesus Christ—He who is the very Son of God Himself.

The following pages explain, explore and apply these last words of the Saviour. In considering them we are given a special insight into the person and work of Christ and are taken into the very heart of the Christian gospel.

Timothy Cross
Cardiff
Wales

A word of
forgiveness

Father, forgive them …

'Jesus Christ and him crucified' (1 Cor. 2:2) lies at the very epicentre of the Christian faith. Crucifixion was a very cruel form of capital punishment practised by the Romans. It entailed its victim being nailed to a plank of wood and hoisted up to die. The physical agony Christ experienced when the Roman soldiers crucified Him cannot be imagined. Yet Christ responded, not by calling out for vengeance on His enemies, but by praying to God for their forgiveness. Christ actually had 'more than twelve legions of angels' (Matt. 26:53) at His disposal. These could have, at His command, meted out the most merciless punishment on both the Roman soldiers who supervised His crucifixion and the Jewish authorities who handed Him over to be crucified. Instead, though, Christ prayed. His first words from the cross were words of mercy: 'Father, forgive them; for they know not what they do' (Luke 23:34).

In His famous Sermon on the Mount, Christ enjoined His disciples to 'Love your enemies and pray for those who persecute you' (Matt. 5:44). Christ's first words from Calvary reveal that He practised what He preached. Christ was characterized by non-retaliation. Years later, Peter recalled how 'When he was reviled, he did not revile in return; when he suffered, he did not threaten; but he trusted to him who judges justly' (1 Peter 2:23).

The gospel of forgiveness

Christ's first words from the cross were, therefore, words of forgiveness: 'Father, forgive …' His words have an infinitely wider application than their immediate context, because the forgiveness of sins is at the very heart of the Christian gospel. Divine forgiveness is central to Christian salvation. The forgiveness of sins is 'music in the sinner's ears'[1] indeed; it is a blessing known to Christians alone and makes the Christian gospel the good news that it is. The Christian gospel proclaims that, in the eternal plan of God, the Lord Jesus Christ died to procure the believing sinner's forgiveness:

> He died that we might be forgiven,
> He died to make us good;
> That we might go at last to heaven,
> Saved by His precious blood.[2]

The verb 'to forgive' means to pardon, remit, cancel the debt, refrain from inflicting the punishment deserved. 'Forgiveness' is the resultant state of blessedness from being forgiven. Forgiveness is a synonym for salvation. 'Forgiven' may be written on every believer's grave.

The brightness of the gospel of forgiveness, however, makes no sense at all unless it is preached against the dark background of human sin. We need to be forgiven. According to the Bible we are all sinners, both by nature and by practice. 'Surely there is not a righteous man on earth who does good and never sins' (Eccles. 7:20). The *Westminster Shorter Catechism* defines sin as 'any want of conformity unto, or transgression of, the law of

God'.[3] It is when we are enabled to realize that sin is ultimately committed against Almighty God Himself that we grasp both its seriousness and its eternal consequences. Sin puts us in God's debt. Sin renders us deserving of God's punishment. Sin, being rebellion against God, robs Him of His honour and robs us of the fellowship with Him which is our chief end and true joy.

The good news of the gospel, however, proclaims that there is forgiveness for all who put their faith in the crucified Saviour. His first words at Calvary were 'Father, forgive ...' It is precisely because Jesus died in the sinner's place at Calvary that Almighty God is able to forgive our sins. He is able to forgive us our sins because Jesus bore them there on the cross. In 1 Peter 2:24 we read, 'He himself bore our sins in his body on the tree.' He was punished by God for our sins so that we, by believing in Him, may know the pardon of God for our sins. At Calvary, He was condemned so that we might be acquitted. He suffered the wrath of God for our sins so that we might be saved from it. Jesus, the sinless Son of God, died, not for His own sins, but for the sins of others. His death was substitutionary. His death was propitiatory. 'Christ died for *our* sins ...' (1 Cor. 15:3);[4] He 'was put to death for *our* trespasses' (Rom. 4:25).

Around 700 BC, Isaiah the prophet gave a detailed prophecy concerning the death of Christ at Calvary. He concluded by saying that Christ both 'bore the sin of many, and made intercession for the transgressors' (Isa. 53:12). The prophecy was most wonderfully fulfilled. Christ did indeed die for the sins of others at Calvary. And Christ did indeed make intercession for sinners at Calvary, when He prayed, 'Father, forgive them ...'

The *Apostles' Creed* is an early summary of the non-negotiables of the Christian faith. Notably it includes the line 'I believe in ... the forgiveness of sins'. The forgiveness of our sins through the shedding of Christ's blood at Calvary is not a facet of the gospel; it is actually the very Christian gospel itself. Paul could write, 'In him we have redemption through his blood, the forgiveness of our trespasses, according to the riches of his grace' (Eph. 1:7). John the Apostle wrote, 'I am writing to you, little children, because your sins are forgiven for his sake' (1 John 2:12).

Thank God, then, that Christ died for sinners at Calvary. Thank God that He sent His only Son, 'not to condemn the world, but that the world might be saved through him' (John 3:17). Thank God that Christ's first words on the cross were a prayer, not for retribution or judgement, but for forgiveness. John Calvin wrote, 'It is on the foundation of the remission of sins that our salvation is built and stands ... Christ has Himself purchased the remission of sins and paid for it with the price of His own blood.'[5]

Reflect on these points

1. *The physical agony Christ experienced when the Roman soldiers crucified Him cannot be imagined. Yet Christ responded, not by calling out for vengeance on His enemies, but by praying to God for their forgiveness.*

2. *We are all sinners, both by nature and by practice, and our sin is ultimately committed against Almighty God Himself. The good news of the gospel, however, proclaims that there is forgiveness for all who put their faith in the crucified Saviour.*

3. *Divine forgiveness is central to Christian salvation. It is a blessing known to Christians alone and makes the Christian gospel the good news that it is.*

ENDNOTES ➤

Endnotes

1 Charles Wesley, 'O For a Thousand Tongues to Sing', 1739.

2 C. F. Alexander, 'There Is a Green Hill Far Away', 1848.

3 *Westminster Shorter Catechism*, answer to Question 14: 'What is sin?'

4 All emphasis in Scripture quotes has been added.

5 John Calvin, *Truth for All Time: A Brief Outline of the Christian Faith,* trans. Stuart Olyott (Edinburgh: Banner of Truth, 1998), p. 46.

A word of forgiveness

A word of promise

Truly, I say to you, today you will be with me in Paradise.

Luke 23:43

Saved by grace alone

Christ's cross was not the only cross at Calvary. Scripture records that 'two robbers were crucified with him, one on the right and one on the left' (Matt. 27:38), with 'Jesus between them' (John 19:18). One of these two criminals rejected Christ and so is eternally lost. The other, however, was enabled to turn to Christ in faith and so is eternally saved. Christ promised him a home in 'Paradise'. Paradise refers to a place of bliss and rest in the nearer presence of God. This saved criminal is, therefore, a wonderful example of salvation by the sheer grace of God. In the morning he was a condemned criminal. In the afternoon he was a redeemed sinner. In the evening he was a glorified saint—with Christ, in Paradise. By merits he deserved a place in perdition, but by the mercy of God in Christ he gained a place in Paradise. He deserved to be in hell, but Christ granted him a place in heaven. His journey from the gallows to the glory is inexplicable apart from divine grace, just as the salvation of any one of us is inexplicable apart from the sovereign, saving grace of God—that is, the unmerited favour and kindness of God to the undeserving and ill-deserving. Salvation by divine grace is the touchstone of authentic biblical Christianity. 'For by grace you have been saved through faith; and this is not your own doing, it is the

gift of God, not because of works, lest any man should boast'
(Eph. 2:8–9).

The steps to glory

The redeemed, dying thief hails from a different background
and era from ours. Yet facets of his salvation transcend the
ages. There are elements in his journey to glory which are
common to every instance of divine salvation.

First of all, the saved, dying thief feared God. Whereas his
partner in crime railed against Christ, this man 'rebuked him,
saying, "Do you not fear God …?"' (Luke 23:40). Scripture
states that 'The fear of the LORD is the beginning of wisdom'
(Prov. 9:10). Impending death, the prospect of eternity and
an imminent facing of divine judgement have, under God,
softened many a hard heart and inculcated in many the
fear of God—a fear which is the necessary prerequisite and
preliminary to salvation.

Secondly, this saved, dying thief was enabled to realize
both his own nature and Christ's nature. He realized his own
sinfulness and Christ's sinlessness: 'we are receiving the due
reward of our deeds; but this man has done nothing wrong'
(Luke 23:41). Luther is said to have commented that 'an
awareness of sin is the beginning of salvation'. Only the Holy
Spirit can convict us of our personal sin and lost plight, and of
our deep and desperate need to be right with God. The Holy
Spirit was thus evidently at work in the thief's heart—albeit at
the last hour.

The thief confessed, '… this man has done nothing

wrong.' The New Testament is uniform in its testimony to Christ's absolute sinlessness—His impeccability. The New Testament also states that 'the wages of sin is death' (Rom. 6:23). Christ was thus dying not for His own sins but for the sins of others. 'Christ also died for sins once for all, the righteous for the unrighteous, that he might bring us to God' (1 Peter 3:18).

Thirdly, the dying thief was enabled to realize not just Christ's sinlessness, but also His authority to bestow salvation. His eyes were opened to Christ's kingdom of grace. There is a kingdom of the redeemed which is ruled by Christ—and the dying thief earnestly wanted to be a subject of it. He thus turned to Christ and begged for mercy, saying, 'Jesus, remember me when you come into your kingdom' (Luke 23:42).

The thief was in a state of double jeopardy. Not only was he a criminal condemned by Rome, but he was also a sinner under the condemnation of God—as indeed we all are by nature. He had no personal merit to plead. He could only plead for mercy. And so he turned to the Lord Jesus and simply asked to be remembered by Him. It was a simple request—but to be remembered by Jesus is abundantly and eternally enough.

The dying thief turned repentantly to Jesus. While we are not saved by repentance—Christ alone saves—paradoxically, there is also no salvation without repentance—that is, turning in faith to Christ. 'Repentance unto life is a saving grace, whereby a sinner, out of a true sense of his sin, and apprehension of the mercy of God in Christ, doth, with grief and hatred of his sin, turn from it unto God, with full purpose of, and endeavour after, new obedience.'[1] Repentance has been termed 'the tear of faith'. Repentance is a gift from God.

Fourthly, we note the promise which Jesus made. The promise of Jesus to every sinner who turns to Him is: 'him who comes to me I will not [lit. 'never, never'] cast out' (John 6:37). This then takes us to our second word of Christ from the cross. Jesus gave the dying thief a gracious and wonderful word of promise: 'Truly, I say to you, today you will be with me in Paradise' (Luke 23:43). Jesus, as the Son of God, always keeps His word. His promises are dependable. Thus, that very day, the thief went from agony to ecstasy, from the gallows to the glory. The Bible is restrained in its description of Paradise, the place of blessedness which awaits the believer. We can, though, say that Paradise entails being 'with *me*'—that is, with Christ our Saviour—for all eternity. Truly, then, for those who belong to Jesus, 'to die is gain' (Phil. 1:21). We can say with Paul, 'My desire is to depart and be with Christ, for that is far better' (Phil. 1:23).

The dying thief depended—and could depend—on Christ's word of promise. And it is the same for every believer today. Our salvation rests on the firm foundation of the Word of God Himself—that 'God has not destined us for wrath, but to obtain salvation through our Lord Jesus Christ' (1 Thes. 5:9).

The Bible says, 'He who believes in the Son has eternal life' (John 3:36).

The saved, dying thief was certainly a trophy of divine grace, a vessel of mercy. Yet every believer can relate to him. The same grace and mercy of God in Christ which saved him has also saved us. When we reach Paradise, it would be wonderful if we could seek out the dying thief and sing a duet with him. Together, we could testify,

> Naught have I gotten, but what I received;
> Grace hath bestowed it and I have believed;
> Boasting excluded, pride I abase;
> I'm only a sinner saved by grace!
>
> *Only a sinner saved by grace!*
> *Only a sinner saved by grace!*
> *This is my story, to God be the glory,*
> *I'm only a sinner, saved by grace!*[2]

REFLECTION POINTS ➤

Reflect on these points

1. *In the morning, this man was a condemned criminal. In the afternoon, he was a redeemed sinner. In the evening, he was a glorified saint—with Christ, in Paradise. He deserved to be in hell, but Christ granted him a place in heaven.*

2. *Impending death, the prospect of eternity and an imminent facing of divine judgement have, under God, softened many a hard heart and inculcated in many the fear of God—a fear which is the necessary prerequisite and preliminary to salvation.*

3. *There is no salvation without repentance—that is, turning in faith to Christ.*

4. *Jesus, as the Son of God, always keeps His word. His promises are dependable. Our salvation rests on the firm foundation of the Word of God Himself.*

Endnotes

1 *Westminster Shorter Catechism,* answer to Question 87: 'What is repentance unto life?'

2 James Gray, 1851–1935.

A word of
compassion

Woman, behold, your son! … Behold, your mother!

John 19:26–27

Aaron—God's anointed high priest in the time of Moses—used to wear a special breastplate on which twelve precious stones were set. On these twelve stones the names of the twelve tribes of Israel were engraved. The whole of Israel was thus literally on Aaron's heart when he went into the holy place of the tabernacle to meet with God and offer sacrifice and intercede for the people. 'So Aaron shall bear the names of the sons of Israel in the breastpiece of judgment upon his heart, when he goes into the holy place, to bring them to continual remembrance before the LORD' (Exod. 28:29).

When Christ our 'great high priest' (Heb. 4:14) offered up His sinless life as an atoning sacrifice at Calvary, all of God's elect people, delineated by Jesus as 'all whom thou hast given him' (John 17:2), were on His heart. God's elect, chosen by Him, redeemed by Christ and sanctified by the Spirit, are 'a great multitude which no man could number' (Rev. 7:9). They transcend both the nations and the ages. Yet this great number did not detract the Saviour from a special concern for one particular person: Mary, His earthly mother.

Mary's distress

It is likely that Joseph, Mary's husband and Jesus' legal guardian, died during Jesus' childhood, for we read no more of him after the incident in Luke 2:41–52, when the Lord was twelve years old. Mary was therefore in a vulnerable position. She lacked a husband's support and care, and she now had to endure the horror of her firstborn son's crucifixion. While dying to procure the salvation of God's elect, therefore, the Lord Jesus took a moment to care for His mother, ensuring that her physical and psychological needs were provided for by the Apostle John. John was guided by the Holy Spirit to record this fact in his Gospel: 'But standing by the cross of Jesus [was] his mother … When Jesus saw his mother, and the disciple whom he loved standing near, he said to his mother, "Woman, behold, your son!" Then he said to the disciple, "Behold, your mother!" And from that hour the disciple took her to his own home' (John 19:25–27). Christ's personal agony and concern for God's elect notwithstanding, Mary was now safely under the care and the roof of the Apostle John, thanks to the word of Jesus.

Not long after Jesus' birth, an aged man named Simeon had prophesied to Mary, 'Behold, this child is set for the fall and rising of many in Israel … (and a sword will pierce through your own soul also) …' (Luke 2:34–35). Simeon's prophecy was fulfilled at Calvary. Mary's anguish was surely beyond human imagination. Seeing her firstborn son being cruelly nailed to a plank of wood and then hung up to die was truly akin to a sword being driven through her very soul. Knowing her plight, the Lord Jesus intervened. Even though He was suffering intensely Himself, He ensured that Mary His mother was entrusted to the care of a trusted friend, John, the 'beloved disciple'. John was Jesus' gracious provision for Mary in her hour of deepest need. Mary was now John's responsibility.

The law of God

The fifth commandment—part of the moral law of God, binding for all time—states, 'Honour your father and your mother, that your days may be long in the land which the LORD your God gives you' (Exod. 20:12). Regarding Jesus' earthly parents, it is written that He 'was obedient to them' (Luke 2:51) as a child. This incident on the cross reveals that the Saviour honoured His earthly parents up until His dying breath. Christ alone of the children of men kept the law of God fully and perfectly. It was His complete obedience to God's law which qualified Him to redeem sinners from the curse of the law— from the dreadful and damnable consequences of disobedience to God's law. Jesus' life and ministry are all of a piece. He lived a sinless life and He died an atoning death. 'Christ redeemed us from the curse of the law, having become a curse for us—for it is written, "Cursed be every one who hangs on a tree"' (Gal. 3:13). Christ's obedience to the law of God thus has both active and passive facets. Actively, He fulfilled God's law. Passively, on behalf of others, He suffered the curse of breaking God's law, so that all law-breakers who believe in Him might be saved from that curse.

Christ cared for His earthly mother. Here the Redeemer gives an example to the redeemed. Calvin explains the fifth commandment thus:

By this commandment we are instructed to exercise piety towards our fathers and mothers ... That is to say, that we are to show them respect, obedience and thankfulness, and to render to them every service possible. For it is the Lord's will that we should act like this to those who have given us life ... they have been given to us as father and mother by the Lord, who has willed that we should honour them.[1]

Forward to the resurrection

'Woman, behold, your son! ... Behold, your mother!' John, as it were, now took the place of Jesus in Mary's life. He was now Mary's adopted son, and Mary was his adopted mother. John witnessed the Lord's death—but John also witnessed the Lord's resurrection three days later. Running to the tomb with Peter, he saw Christ's undisturbed grave clothes inside, 'the linen cloths lying there' (John 20:5). Scripture states that John 'went in, and he saw and believed' (John 20:8). 'Then the disciples went back to their homes' (20:10). Let us put two verses side by side and put an emphasis on the common word 'home':

> And from that hour the disciple took her to his own *home* (John 19:27).

> Then the disciples went back to their *homes* (John 20:10).

Who, then, was at John's home when he returned there,

believing and rejoicing in Christ's conquest of the grave? Mary was! Scripture is silent, but how could John not but exclaim that Christ's tomb was empty and that He had risen from the dead!

In later centuries, Mary received a prominence in Christendom not sanctioned by Scripture. Scripture does, however, honour her as the earthly mother of the Saviour. The Saviour Himself honoured her by entrusting her earthly care to the Apostle John. The last we read of 'Mary the mother of Jesus' is in Acts 1:14. There we see her taking her place in the Christian community. She herself was never worshipped; rather, she joined in with the worship of the church. And the object of her and their worship was the Lord Jesus Christ, He who is both the Son of Mary and the Son of God, who died and rose again to save sinners. Jesus was Mary's special child but also her superlative Saviour. He is the Saviour of all who put their trust in Him.

> Lord Jesus Christ,
> You have come to us,
> Born as one of us,
> Mary's son;
> Led out to die on Calvary,
> Risen from death to set us free,
> Living Lord Jesus, help us see
> You are Lord.[2]

Reflect on these points

1. *When Christ offered up His sinless life as an atoning sacrifice at Calvary, all of God's elect people were on His heart. Yet this great number did not detract from His special concern for one particular person: Mary, His earthly mother.*

2. *The Saviour honoured His earthly parents up until His dying breath. Christ alone of the children of men kept the law of God fully and perfectly.*

3. *Christ's obedience to the law of God had both active and passive facets. Actively, He fulfilled God's law. Passively, on behalf of others, He suffered the curse of breaking God's law, so that all law-breakers who believe in Him might be saved from that curse.*

Endnotes

1 Calvin, *Truth for All Time*, pp. 17–18.

2 Patrick Appleford, b. 1925.

A cry of dereliction

My God, my God, why hast thou forsaken me?

Matt. 27:46

Christ's cry of dereliction, the fourth of His seven sayings from the cross, is the central saying. It is, however, central in more ways than one. His being momentarily forsaken by His Father reveals that He was bearing His Father's wrath. The word for this is 'propitiation'. To 'propitiate' means to appease, to satisfy, to turn wrath aside. Christ's propitiatory work at Calvary could not be more central to the Christian gospel. 'In this is love, not that we loved God but that he loved us and sent his Son to be the propitiation[1] for our sins' (1 John 4:10).

The Gospel records reveal that when Christ died on Calvary's cross He experienced both darkness and dereliction. His dereliction was expressed by Him vocally. Matthew's account states, 'Now from the sixth hour there was darkness over all the land until the ninth hour. And about the ninth hour Jesus cried with a loud voice, "Eli, Eli, la'ma sabach-tha'ni?" that is, "My God, my God, why hast thou forsaken me?"' (Matt. 27:45–46). The darkness and the dereliction of Calvary are linked; they are two sides of one coin, as we shall see.

John Calvin stated that in the redemption procured by Christ at Calvary 'there is nothing that is without mystery'.[2] We are dealing here with the very heart of the Christian gospel and one of the great profundities of the Christian faith. A reverent caution thus becomes us in our explanation.

The darkness

The darkness of Calvary occurred in the springtime from midday until 3 p.m. This darkness is inexplicable apart from an act of God:

> Well might the sun in darkness hide
> And shut his glories in
> When God, the mighty Maker died
> For man, the creature's sin.[3]

In the Bible, darkness signifies divine judgement. At the time of the redemption from Egypt, God sent three days of darkness as a judgement on Pharaoh: 'there was thick darkness in all the land of Egypt three days' (Exod. 10:22). Jesus Himself described hell, the ultimate in divine judgement, as 'the outer darkness; there men will weep and gnash their teeth' (Matt. 8:12).

The darkness of Calvary therefore reveals that the Lord Jesus was experiencing divine judgement there. He was actually being punished by His Father, not for His own sins—for He had none—but for the sins of others. The condemning judgement He suffered at Calvary was a substitutionary one; it was borne in the place of others. He was judged so that we, by believing in Him, might be justified—declared 'not guilty'—in God's sight. He was punished so that we might be pardoned. He experienced the 'outer darkness' so that we might 'share in the inheritance of the saints in light' and be 'delivered … from the dominion of darkness and transferred … to the kingdom of his beloved Son' (Col. 1:12–13). The substitutionary nature of Christ's death—that He died in the place of sinners to save sinners—is surely revealed by the darkness of Calvary just as it is revealed further, and formidably, in His cry of dereliction.

The dereliction

'My God, my God, why hast thou forsaken me?' (Matt. 27:46). The Saviour here was quoting from Psalm 22:1. This psalm was written by David around 1000 BC, but nothing in it seems to tally with David's known life. The psalm was prophetic of 'great David's greater Son', even down to the details. Verses 16–18, for instance, say, '… they have pierced my hands and feet—I can count all my bones—they stare and gloat over me; they divide my garments among them, and for my raiment they cast lots.' Here is a psalm which foretold Christ's death at Calvary—inexplicable apart from divine inspiration.

Christ's fourth word from the cross was, then, a cry of dereliction. The 'cup' of suffering which He anticipated in Gethsemane was now being drunk and drained fully. Christ was forsaken by His Father, and so He cried out, 'My God, my God, why hast thou forsaken me?' The question is, 'Why indeed?' It was because the sins of God's elect had been imputed to Christ, and sin is an affront to a holy God. The Bible states that, on the cross, the sinless Christ was actually 'made sin': 'For our sake he made him to be sin who knew no sin, so that in him we might become the righteousness of God' (2 Cor. 5:21). 'He himself bore our sins in his body on the tree' (1 Peter 2:24). Almighty God is 'of purer eyes than to behold evil and canst not look on wrong' (Hab. 1:13). And so, when

His beloved Son bore our sins at Calvary, God could only turn aside from Him. Bearing our sins, Christ momentarily lost the unalloyed fellowship He had always known and enjoyed with His Father. He did this so that believing sinners could enjoy that fellowship with Him for all eternity. His forsakenness was for believers' forgiveness. His judgement was for our justification. His dereliction was for our deliverance. He was alienated from God so that sinners might be reconciled to God. His abandonment procured our atonement.

Christ's cry of dereliction, therefore, truly takes us to the very heart of the gospel, to the centre of the redeeming plan of God. His fourth word was indeed His central saying from the cross. Christ's living was with a view to His dying. His coming to earth was specifically for these three dark, last hours. He literally tasted hell, that 'we might go at last to heaven, saved by His precious blood'[4].

> He was struck by God and ... endured and felt the horrible rigours of God's judgement, putting Himself between God's anger and ourselves, and satisfying God's justice on our behalf. He thus suffered and bore the punishment which our unrighteousness deserved, while there was not the slightest trace of sin in Him ... He bore the weight of God's anger in the sense of being struck and overcome by the hand of God, He experienced all the expressions of God's fury and retribution to the point of being moved to

cry out in anguish 'My God, my God, why have you
abandoned me?'[5]

The Holy One did hide His face;
O Christ, 'twas hid from Thee:
Dumb darkness wrapped Thy soul a space,
The darkness due to me.
But now that face of radiant grace
Shines forth in light on me.[6]

REFLECTION POINTS ➤

Reflect on these points

1. *When Christ died on Calvary's cross He experienced both darkness and dereliction. We are dealing here with the very heart of the Christian gospel and one of the great profundities of the Christian faith.*

2. *The darkness of Calvary reveals that the Lord Jesus was experiencing divine judgement there. He was actually being punished by His Father, not for His own sins—for He had none—but for the sins of others.*

3. *He was judged so that we, by believing in Him, might be justified in God's sight. He was punished so that we might be pardoned.*

4. *When His beloved Son bore our sins at Calvary, God could only turn aside from Him. Bearing our sins, Christ momentarily lost the unalloyed fellowship He had always known and enjoyed with His Father.*

Endnotes

1 'Propitiation' is my translation of the Greek word *hilasmos*; rsv uses 'expiation'.

2 Calvin, *Truth for All Time,* p. 40.

3 Isaac Watts, 1707–1709, 'Alas! and Did My Saviour Bleed'.

4 Alexander, 'There Is a Green Hill Far Away'.

5 Calvin, *Truth for All Time,* pp. 40–41.

6 Anne Ross Cousin, 1824–1906.

A word of need

I thirst.

John 19:28

It is understandable that the Lord Jesus experienced a terrible, raging thirst while He hung on the cross. He had suffered much blood loss, and before the unusual noontime darkness, when 'the sun's light failed' (Luke 23:45; or 'was eclipsed', margin), He had been hanging there in the fierce heat, as the sun beat down on a cloudless Middle Eastern day. Thirst is one of the most unpleasant and uncomfortable of human conditions and, if untreated, is fatal. The Lord Jesus experienced this on the cross. In His extremely dehydrated state He thus expressed a word of need: 'I thirst.'

John notes that Jesus' expression of physical need—'I thirst'—was said 'to fulfil the scripture' (John 19:28). Some thousand years previously, the 'Calvary Psalm' had foretold Christ's thirst. David, under the inspiration of the Holy Spirit, was enabled to give an 'insider's view' of Calvary, with the words 'I am poured out like water, and all my bones are out of joint; my heart is like wax, it is melted within my breast; my strength is dried up like a potsherd, and my tongue cleaves to my jaws; thou dost lay me in the dust of death' (Ps. 22:14–15). Scripture also records that a compassionate, anonymous person—possibly a soldier—took it upon himself to alleviate Jesus' thirst: 'And one of them at once ran and took a sponge, filled it with vinegar, and put it on a reed, and gave it to him to drink' (Matt. 27:48). This also was a fulfilment of Scripture, for in Psalm 69:21 we read, '... for my thirst they gave me vinegar to drink.'

Physical thirst

There were those in the early church who denied that Christ was truly human. They were known as 'Docetists', from the Greek verb 'to seem'. Christ only *seemed* to be human, they taught. Christ's intense thirst, however, reveals that His humanity was real. In Christ, God became man. 'For in him the whole fullness of deity dwells bodily' (Col. 2:9). Scripture reveals His real humanity as much as His absolute deity. The Gospel records show that Christ wept (John 11:35)—showing that He had human emotion—and that He slept (Mark 4:38). John 4:6 reveals that He experienced fatigue: 'Jesus, wearied as he was with his journey, sat down beside the well.' Jesus also experienced the psychological pain of mockery and ridicule (Matt. 27:27–31). Our title verse shows that He experienced physical thirst.

From all this evidence revealing Christ's real humanity, we can state that in Christ we have a God who really does understand what it is like to be human. In Christ we have a sympathetic Saviour, well acquainted with physical, psychological, social and spiritual suffering. 'For we have not a high priest who is unable to sympathize with our weaknesses, but one who in every respect has been tempted as we are, yet without sin' (Heb. 4:15):

> Our fellow-sufferer yet retains
> A fellow-feeling of our pains;

And still remembers in the skies
His tears, His agonies and cries.

In every pang that rends the heart,
The Man of Sorrows had a part;
He sympathizes with our grief,
And to the sufferer sends relief.[1]

Spiritual thirst

'I thirst.' We can consider Christ's word of need on more than just a physical level. Thirst signifies a desire and craving. Thirst can thus be more than physical. The Bible reveals the phenomenon of spiritual thirst—the thirst of the soul; the desire for fellowship with God our Maker; the desire to realize our 'chief end', which is 'to glorify God, and to enjoy Him for ever'.[2] Hence the psalmist could write, 'As a hart longs for flowing streams, so longs my soul for thee, O God. My soul thirsts for God, for the living God' (Ps. 42:1–2); and '... my soul thirsts for thee; my flesh faints for thee, as in a dry and weary land where no water is' (Ps. 63:1).

Christ the eternal Son of God had enjoyed exquisite fellowship with His Father in eternity past, along with the joy of unalloyed fellowship with His Father during the whole of His life on earth. Until this point. On the cross, when He bore our sin and God's anger on it, He was, momentarily, cut off from the unblemished fellowship with His Father He had always known. Sin separates us from God; 'your iniquities have made a separation between you and your God, and your sins have hid his face from you' (Isa. 59:2). When our sins were imputed to Christ, He was separated from His Father. Christ thus experienced an intense spiritual thirst on the cross, as well as a physical one. He thirsted for the fellowship with His Father which He had lost. And He thirsted so that the believing sinner will never suffer spiritual thirst.

The ultimate in spiritual thirst is hell itself. Hell is, among other things, a thirst for God that will never be quenched for all eternity. Jesus once told of a man in hell who desired someone 'to dip the end of his finger in water and cool my tongue; for I am in anguish in this flame' (Luke 16:24). The thirst of hell truly made it a 'place of torment' (16:28) for that condemned man.

On the cross, Christ experienced hell in the sinner's place, so that the sinner might go at last to heaven. On the cross, Christ thirsted. He thirsted so that a fountain of living water could be opened for thirsty sinners. Trusting the crucified Christ sees us having our sins forgiven and our fellowship with God restored. Trusting Christ means having our spiritual thirst quenched for time and eternity. On Calvary He thirsted to save sinners from eternal thirst. Jesus thus still extends the promise to sinners: 'If any one thirst, let him come to me and drink. He who believes in me, as the scripture has said, "Out of his heart shall flow rivers of living water"' (John 7:37–38).

The closing verses of the Bible hold out a wonderful invitation to all who are aware of their spiritual thirst. The invitation is: Come to Jesus and drink! 'And let him who is thirsty come, let him who desires take the water of life without price' (Rev. 22:17). Salvation entails deliverance from the thirst of hell. Paradoxically, just as the 'light of the world' (John 8:12) experienced darkness at Calvary so that sinners might live in God's eternal light, so, on the cross, Jesus cried, 'I thirst.' He thirsted so that the sinner's thirst might be quenched for ever.

> I heard the voice of Jesus say,
> 'Behold, I freely give
> The living water; thirsty one,
> Stoop down and drink and live!'
> I came to Jesus and I drank
> Of that life-giving stream:
> My thirst was quenched, my soul revived,
> And now I live in Him.[3]

REFLECTION POINTS ➤

Reflect on these points

1. *In Christ we have a God who really does understand what it is like to be human. In Christ we have a sympathetic Saviour, well acquainted with physical, psychological, social and spiritual suffering.*

2. *The Bible reveals the phenomenon of spiritual thirst— the thirst of the soul; the desire for fellowship with God our Maker. Christ experienced an intense spiritual thirst on the cross, as well as a physical one. He thirsted for the fellowship with His Father which He had lost. And He thirsted so that the believing sinner will never suffer spiritual thirst.*

3. *Hell is, among other things, a thirst for God that will never be quenched for all eternity.*

4. *The closing verses of the Bible hold out a wonderful invitation to all who are aware of their spiritual thirst: Come to Jesus and drink!*

Endnotes

1 Michael Bruce, 1746–1767, 'Where High the Heavenly Temple Stands'.

2 *Westminster Shorter Catechism,* answer to Question 1: 'What is the chief end of man?'

3 Horatius Bonar, 1846.

A shout of triumph

It is finished.

Born to die

The life of Christ was like that of no other. His teaching, miracles and sinless character were incomparable. Remarkably, however, Scripture teaches that Christ accomplished far more by His death than by His life. 'Christ Jesus came into the world to save sinners' (1 Tim. 1:15), and it was by His atoning death on Calvary's cross that the sinner's salvation was actually and eternally procured.

The Lord Jesus Christ was about thirty-three years old when He died. Death at such an early age would normally be viewed as a terrible and sad calamity. Christ's death, however, was not a tragedy but a triumph. Christ's death was no accident but an accomplishment. He was not a victim but a Victor. And this is brought out by Christ's sixth word from the cross. With a shout of triumph, He proclaimed, 'It is finished' (John 19:30).

Christ's parched mouth, due to His raging thirst, made speech difficult. The welcome drink of wine vinegar, though, moistened His mouth and enabled Him to speak clearly. John the Apostle's vivid, eyewitness account thus records, 'When Jesus had received the vinegar, he said, "It is finished"; and he bowed his head and gave up his spirit' (John 19:30).

'It is finished.' The words take us to the very heart of the Christian gospel and the sure foundation of the Christian's eternal salvation, for they take us to 'the finished work of Christ on the cross':

> 'Tis finished! The Messiah dies,
> Cut off for sins, but not His own;
> Accomplished is the sacrifice,
> The great redeeming work is done.

> 'Tis finished! All the debt is paid;
> Justice divine is satisfied;
> The great and full atonement made;
> Christ for a guilty world hath died.[1]

A perfect work

'It is finished.' These three words are actually just one word in the original Greek of the Bible. The word is *tetelestai*. The verb employed by the Holy Spirit is in the perfect tense referring to a present state resulting from a past action, or an action in the past with abiding consequences in the present. Christ's death was, therefore, no ordinary death. The sacrifice of the eternal Son of God has eternal, abiding, saving consequences. We could paraphrase Christ's shout of triumph in the following ways:

- 'I have accomplished the eternal salvation of God's people.'
- 'I have paid the debt of my people's sin in full.'
- 'I have fulfilled all the types, shadows and prophecies of the coming Redeemer foretold in Scripture.'

- 'I have wrought the forgiveness of my people's sins so that they will remain eternally forgiven.'
- 'I have made full atonement for my people.'
- 'My sacrifice has put an end to all sacrifice, and rendered the sacrificial priesthood redundant.'
- 'I have completed the work which my Father sent me to do in His eternal plan.'
- Or, to employ Christ's own words, 'I glorified thee on earth, having accomplished the work which thou gavest me to do' (John 17:4).

The heart of our faith

Christ's words 'It is finished' lie at the very heart of the Christian faith. They draw our attention to His perfect work of redemption at Calvary. Perfection, by its nature, can neither be improved upon nor diminished. Nothing can add to or subtract from what Christ achieved at Calvary. From Calvary's cross flows the believer's eternal salvation. 'But when Christ had offered for all time a single sacrifice for sins, he sat down at the right hand of God' (Heb. 10:12). The secret of Christian assurance is surely to look away from ourselves and to focus our attention on the all-prevailing sufficiency of the finished work of Christ. It is His great work that saves us—nothing more, nothing less and nothing else. Jesus is the eternal Son of God. His blood has power to atone. His perfect sacrifice is able to save us eternally. He is our all-sufficient Saviour who has averted the wrath of God from us. Salvation depends on His work, not on our works.

Implications

The 'finished work of Christ' exposes the folly of salvation by human works and endeavour. 'Salvation by works' seeks to add to—but actually detracts from—the perfection of what Christ has done. There were those in Paul's day who, by their religious works, tarnished and detracted from Christ's cross-work, just as there are today. Paul's rejoinder then is just as applicable today: 'I do not nullify the grace of God; for if justification were through the law, then Christ died to no purpose' (Gal. 2:21).

The 'finished work of Christ' is a needed reminder that it is His great work—and His work alone—that can save a lost sinner. The aim of Christian evangelism is therefore, under God, to get sinners to the foot of the cross. Faith in the crucified Saviour is the gospel imperative, as Scripture states that there is salvation in no one else (Acts 4:12). Salvation rests solely on the finished work of Christ. It is wholly and solely 'of the Lord'. It is not a matter of 'do' but of what Christ has already *done*. Praise God, 'It is finished'!

> Nothing either great or small,
> Nothing, sinner, no;
> Jesus did it, did it all
> Long, long ago.

> *'It is finished!' yes, indeed;*
> *Finished every jot;*
> *Sinner, this is all you need—*
> *Tell me, is it not?*

When He from His lofty throne
Stooped to do and die,
Everything was fully done;
Hearken to His cry!

Till to Jesus Christ you cling
By a simple faith,
'Doing' is a deadly thing—
'Doing' ends in death.

Cast your deadly 'doing' down—
Down at Jesus' feet;
Stand in Him, in Him alone,
Gloriously complete.[2]

REFLECTION POINTS ➤

Reflect on these points

1. *Christ's death was not a tragedy but a triumph; not an accident but an accomplishment. He was not a victim but a Victor.*

2. *Perfection, by its nature, can neither be improved upon nor diminished. Nothing can add to or subtract from what Christ achieved at Calvary.*

3. *The secret of Christian assurance is to look away from ourselves and to focus our attention on the all-prevailing sufficiency of the finished work of Christ.*

4. *The 'finished work of Christ' is a needed reminder that it is His great work—and His work alone—that can save a lost sinner. The aim of Christian evangelism is therefore, under God, to get sinners to the foot of the cross.*

Endnotes

1 Charles Wesley, 1762.

2 James Proctor, 1864.

A word of
peaceful trust

Father, into thy hands I commit my spirit!

Luke 23:46

The first recorded words of the Lord Jesus are 'Did you not know that I must be in my Father's house?' (Luke 2:49). In the last words of the Lord Jesus on the cross, before He finally expired, He again addressed God as His Father. In words of peaceful repose and trust, He said, 'Father, into thy hands I commit my spirit!' (Luke 23:46). Both these sayings evidence Jesus' unique, divine Sonship. Christians become 'sons of God' by adoption and grace, adoption being one of the New Testament synonyms for salvation. Jesus Himself taught that we should address God, using the words of reverent faith, as 'Our Father who art in heaven' (Matt. 6:9). Christ's Sonship and relation to the Father are, however, altogether different from those of believers. As the second person of the Trinity, He is the unique intrinsic and eternal Son of God. By nature we are not the sons of God, but we may become so through divine, adoptive grace, through Christ the Son of God and God the Son. Christ Himself, however, always was the Son of God.

Steeped in Scripture as the Saviour was, when He uttered the words 'Father, into thy hands I commit my spirit', He was quoting from Psalm 31:5—but quoting it with a significant difference. The full verse reads, 'Into thy hand I commit my spirit, thou hast redeemed me, O LORD, faithful God.' The omission may be explained from the fact that the sinless Redeemer of sinners had no need of being redeemed Himself.

Given, not taken

Luke informs us that the Lord Jesus, 'having said this [that is, these words of peaceful trust] he breathed his last' (Luke 23:46). Scripture is adamant that Christ's life was not actually taken from Him but given by Him. He was in total control. Jesus Himself explained, 'For this reason the Father loves me, because I lay down my life, that I may take it again. No one takes it from me, but I lay it down of my own accord. I have power to lay it down, and I have power to take it again; this charge I have received from my Father' (John 10:17–18). Paul later explained that 'Christ loved the church and gave himself up for her' (Eph. 5:25). Paul also gave a personal testimony common to every Christian when he said that 'the Son of God … loved me and gave himself for me' (Gal. 2:20).

Mission accomplished

'Father, into thy hands I commit my spirit!' Jesus' final words are words of peaceful trust. Having accomplished our salvation, and having entrusted His mother to the care of John, Christ entrusted His soul to God the Father. His soul went to be with Him in glory, while His body was laid lovingly in Joseph of Arimathea's new tomb. Three days later, on the resurrection morning, His soul was reunited with His body when He conquered death and the grave. Interestingly, Scripture states that when He completed the work of creation, God the Father 'rested on the seventh day from all his work which he had done' (Gen. 2:2). Similarly, having completed the work of redemption, God the Son also rested on the seventh day.

The Redeemer and the redeemed

The Redeemer's peaceful repose at His hour of death actually sets a pattern for the redeemed—those who are 'in Christ'. If we belong to Jesus, we need not fear death. It is true that 'The sting of death is sin' (1 Cor. 15:56), but Christ's death on the cross for our sins has taken this sting away from us. Jesus' atoning death has given us an entrance into eternal glory and the right to be there. For the Christian, death is the porter who will usher us into the nearer presence of God, and 'in thy presence there is fullness of joy, in thy right hand are pleasures for evermore' (Ps. 16:11).

When a believer is laid in a grave, it is a matter of their being 'away from the body and at home with the Lord' (2 Cor. 5:8). For the believer, 'to live is Christ, and to die is gain' (Phil. 1:21). And just as Christ's soul was reunited with His body three days after His burial, so likewise, in God's time, all believers' souls will be reunited with their bodies on the Last Day and enter into a new, glorious plane of existence. We will then be able to serve God as we ought, inhabiting our redeemed bodies on a redeemed earth, free from all sorrow, pain and mortality. 'At the resurrection, believers, being raised up in glory, shall be openly acknowledged and acquitted in the day of judgement, and be made perfectly blessed in the full enjoying of God, to all eternity.'[1] For the Christian, the best is yet to be.

The ultimate Christian 'hope'—that is, a confident

expectation and anticipation based on the promises of God—
is not so much the salvation of the soul but the resurrection of
the body. 'Christ has been raised from the dead, the first fruits
of those who have fallen asleep … For as in Adam all die, so
also in Christ shall all be made alive. But each in his own order:
Christ the first fruits, then at his coming those who belong to
Christ' (1 Cor. 15:20, 22–23).

The 'last of Christ's last words' were, then, words of
peaceful trust. 'Father, into thy hands I commit my spirit!' He
entrusted His soul to God the Father with quiet confidence. If
we belong to Jesus and know the salvation which He wrought
at Calvary, we may do the same. Saved by the grace of God in
Christ, we are saved and safe for time and eternity. Nothing at
all, whether in the present or the future, 'will be able to separate
us from the love of God in Christ Jesus our Lord' (Rom. 8:39).

> Teach me to live, that I may dread
> The grave as little as my bed.
> Teach me to die, that so I may
> Rise glorious at the judgement day.
>
> Praise God, from whom all blessings flow;
> Praise Him, all creatures here below;
> Praise Him above, ye heavenly host;
> Praise Father, Son and Holy Ghost.[2]

Reflect on these points

1. *Scripture is adamant that Christ's life was not actually taken from Him but given by Him. He was in total control.*

2. *The Redeemer's peaceful repose at His hour of death sets a pattern for the redeemed. If we belong to Jesus, we need not fear death. Jesus' atoning death has given us an entrance into eternal glory and the right to be there.*

3. *When a believer is laid in a grave, it is a matter of their being 'away from the body and at home with the Lord'. And just as Christ's soul was reunited with His body three days after His burial, so likewise, in God's time, all believers' souls will be reunited with their bodies on the Last Day and enter into a new, glorious plane of existence. For the Christian, the best is yet to be.*

4. *The ultimate Christian 'hope' is not so much the salvation of the soul but the resurrection of the body.*

5. *Christ entrusted His soul to God the Father with quiet confidence. If we belong to Jesus and know the salvation which He wrought at Calvary, we may do the same. Saved by the grace of God in Christ, we are saved and safe for time and eternity. Nothing at all, whether in the present or the future, 'will be able to separate us from the love of God in Christ Jesus our Lord'.*

ENDNOTES ➤

Endnotes

1 *Westminster Shorter Catechism,* answer to Question 38: 'What benefits do believers receive from Christ at the resurrection?'

2 Thomas Ken, 'All Praise to Thee, My God, This Night', 1695.

About Day One:

Day One's threefold commitment:
- To be faithful to the Bible, God's inerrant, infallible Word;
- To be relevant to our modern generation;
- To be excellent in our publication standards.

I continue to be thankful for the publications of Day One. They are biblical; they have sound theology; and they are relevant to the issues at hand. The material is condensed and manageable while, at the same time, being complete—a challenging balance to find. We are happy in our ministry to make use of these excellent publications.

JOHN MACARTHUR, PASTOR-TEACHER, GRACE COMMUNITY CHURCH, CALIFORNIA

It is a great encouragement to see Day One making such excellent progress. Their publications are always biblical, accessible and attractively produced, with no compromise on quality. Long may their progress continue and increase!

JOHN BLANCHARD, AUTHOR, EVANGELIST AND APOLOGIST

Visit our web site for more information and
to request a free catalogue of our books.
www.dayone.co.uk

Also available

Words of encouragement

Messages and Bible studies giving comfort and inspiration

HAROLD K T FAITHFULL

129PP, PAPERBACK

ISBN 978-1-84625-443-7

This book contains a selection of heart-warming messages, sermons, house group Bible studies and prayers from the late Harold Faithfull.

Each message reflects the theme of Encouragement', as well as Harold's personality: his love for God and the gospel of Christ, his conviction of the necessity of absolute obedience to, and trust in, the Saviour, and his deep sympathy for people facing difficulties of all kinds.

Compiled by his son, Nigel, these messages can strengthen believers and enable seekers to find rest and forgiveness for their souls in the Lord Jesus Christ.

I find this book readable and helpful. The brief chapters are useful in that great truths can be quickly grasped and applied. I can see it being of great appeal and use to busy folks who can read just a chapter over a cup of tea and find spiritual refreshment.
REVD DR ANDY CHRISTOFIDES, PASTOR, ST MELLONS BAPTIST CHURCH, CARDIFF, AND AUTHOR OF EVIDENCE FOR GOD AND LIFELINE (DAY ONE)

I feel privileged to write this commendation. Harold Faithfull was everything his surname suggests. He knew the 'deep, deep love of Jesus', and loved Jesus too. I knew him as a mature man, wise, thoughtful and careful. It is all there in this book: a man apprenticed to Christ, committed to reproducing in his own life and deeds the life of his Saviour. Through Harold, many people have felt the influence of Christ on their own lives. A genuinely lovely man, one well worth listening to.
REVD IAN BURLEY MTH, RETIRED PASTOR, UK

When God makes streams in the desert

Revival blessings in the Bible

ROGER ELLSWORTH

128PP, PAPERBACK

ISBN 978-1-84625-176-4

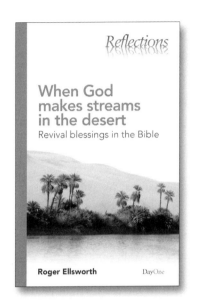

What is biblical revival? Many Christians associate revival with special meetings that used to take place once or twice a year. Guest preachers and singers would be brought in, and special evening services were designed to encourage believers to get closer to the Lord and to convince unbelievers to accept him as their Saviour.

But that is not revival. Biblical revival is about God bringing his people back to spiritual vitality. Only Christians can be revived because only they have spiritual life, having been regenerated by the Spirit of God on the basis of the redeeming work of Christ.

Learn what the Bible teaches about revival, and be inspired to pray that, even in our day, God will make streams flow in the desert!

'With a relentless focus on the Bible itself, Roger Ellsworth reminds us that true revival is a sovereign work of God that radically affects our lives. The best recommendation I can give of this book is that it made me long more intensely and pray more fervently for God to act in the midst of his people.'

CHAD DAVIS, PASTOR, GRACE COMMUNITY CHURCH, MARTIN, TENNESSEE, USA

'When God Makes Streams in the Desert reminds us that revival is present when, as Brian Edwards says, 'remarkable life and power that cannot be explained adequately in any human terms' moves into our churches and causes us to do what we do 'at a different level'. This book will change the way you think about and pray for revival.'

PAUL ORRICK, PASTOR, FIRST BAPTIST CHURCH, GREENVILLE, OHIO, USA

God's good news in the miracles of Jesus

ROGER ELLSWORTH

160PP, PAPERBACK

ISBN 978-1-84625-407-9

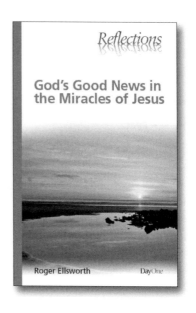

Jesus punctuated his public ministry with astounding deeds. He caused the lame to walk, the blind to see and the deaf to hear. He fed multitudes and stilled storms. He healed the sick and cast out demons. He even raised three people from the dead. And he put the finishing touch on his amazing ministry by rising from his own grave.

As this book demonstrates, all of Jesus's miracles unite their voices to tell us emphatically that we do not have to be in any doubt about his identity. He was none other than God in human flesh, and he came to this earth to provide the way for sinners to be forgiven and to have a right standing with God. His miracles tell us the truth about him and about the salvation he came to provide. That is indeed good news.

This is typical Roger Ellsworth: simple and accurate, pointed and practical, warm and Christ-centred. Further, and very important in a work on Christ's miracles, here are no foolish natural 'explanations', but rather Bible-honouring expositions.

JOHN LEGG, RETIRED PASTOR WITH ITINERANT PREACHING MINISTRY IN SOUTH WALES

As has been stated by many biblical scholars, miracles must be interventions, not movements that continually provide the providential elements of God's decrees. If you want to come back to earth regarding miracle overkill, read this book. It will set your feet on solid ground without the grandstanding of perpetual implication of the miraculous in every event.

ROY HARGRAVE, PASTOR, RIVERBEND COMMUNITY CHURCH, ORMOND BEACH, FLORIDA, USA

God's good news in the parables of Jesus

ROGER ELLSWORTH

160PP, PAPERBACK

ISBN 978-1-84625-408-6

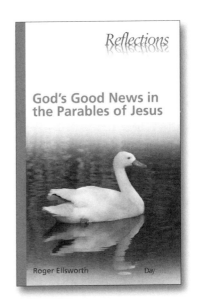

A father's rebellious son leaves home. A man discovers treasure hidden in a field. A woman pesters a judge until he is willing to hear her case. A farmer frets over storing his crop. Drawing from the common experiences of his hearers, Jesus told these and other stories in such riveting fashion that he easily commanded a hearing. But as this book shows, he had a higher purpose than merely to captivate his audiences. These parables were designed to move them from the everyday world to the eternal world and to present them with this good news: that all who truly receive Jesus as Lord and Saviour will live with him in eternal glory.

In brief compass Roger Ellsworth provides clear, sound exposition and application of the parables of Jesus. This volume will be very helpful to pastors and laypeople as they study the Gospels.
RAY VAN NESTE, PROFESSOR OF BIBLICAL STUDIES AND DIRECTOR, R. C. RYAN CENTER FOR BIBLICAL STUDIES, JACKSON, TN, USA

Pastoral wisdom and personal warmth are hallmarks of Roger Ellsworth's commentaries. Reading God's Good News in the Parables of Jesus and reflecting on the various points raised will no doubt encourage greater appreciation of the parables and greater love for Christ.
BARRY KING, GENERAL SECRETARY, GRACE BAPTIST PARTNERSHIP, LONDON

They echoed the voice of God

Reflections on the Minor Prophets

ROGER ELLSWORTH

128PP, PAPERBACK

ISBN 978-1-84625-101-6

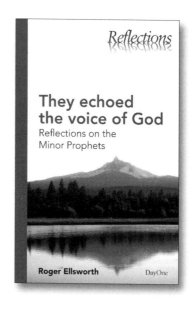

Many carry a little Bible and believe in a little God. Their Bibles are little because they ignore so many of its books. Their God is little because they ignore so many of the Bible's truths. The Minor Prophets can help us. These men made sense of their circumstances and found strength for their challenges by basking in the God who was above it all and in it all. The God they served was wise enough to plan and strong enough to achieve. This study of their messages will help us have both bigger Bibles and a bigger God.

'Roger Ellsworth helps us appreciate how the so-called Minor Prophets make known the character and work of our great God. This book is a great introduction to and overview of their prophecies. Read it to become acquainted with these sometimes overlooked servants and, more importantly, with the unchangeable God whose message they proclaimed.'
TOM ASCOL, DIRECTOR OF FOUNDERS MINISTRIES AND PASTOR, GRACE BAPTIST CHURCH, CAPE CORAL, FLORIDA

'Laced with helpful, practical application, this book shows how each prophet emphasized a particular aspect of God's character, giving an overall picture that is compelling.'
JIM WINTER, MINISTER OF HORSELL EVANGELICAL CHURCH, WOKING

In the care of the Good Shepherd
Meditations on Psalm 23

IAIN D CAMPBELL

112PP, PAPERBACK

ISBN 978-1-84625-175-7

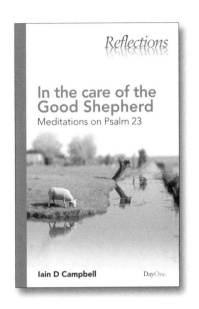

There is probably no passage of Scripture with which people are more familiar than the twenty-third psalm. The words of the metrical version are among the best loved and most often sung of our Scottish Metrical Psalms. Every statement of the psalm is loaded with meaning and with significance and importance. Enjoy reading through these inspiring meditations on Psalm 23.

'Iain D. Campbell's exposition of Psalm 23 is masterful, both exegetically and pastorally. Reminiscent of the late Douglas MacMillan's work on this psalm, Dr Campbell's adds significantly to our appreciation of the psalm; indeed, under his guidance we are led to behold new vistas of greener pastures and still waters. Sure-footed expository genius of a rare kind.'
DEREK THOMAS, REFORMED THEOLOGICAL SEMINARY, JACKSON, MISSISSIPPI, USA

'The book is written by one who functions as an under-shepherd of the Saviour and who is aware of the spiritual needs and desires of his flock, and this experience is very much to the fore throughout the work. Further, the activities of Jesus are described in such a straightforward devotional manner that makes the book a joy to read. It is a book suitable for the heart as well as for the mind.'
REVD DR MALCOLM MACLEAN, MINISTER, SCALPAY FREE CHURCH OF SCOTLAND

Hints and signs of the coming King

Pictures of Jesus in the Old Testament

KURT STRASSNER

112PP, PAPERBACK

ISBN978-1-84625-208-2

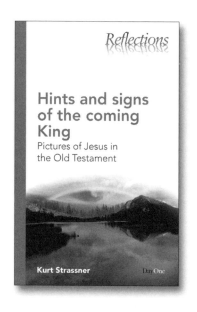

In the Bible, God often paints spiritual concepts with the bright colors of illustration: "Behold, the Lamb of God who takes away the sin of the world" (John 1:29). But it is not just Bible teaching that can be metaphoric; Bible events can be, too. God often worked out Bible history—real events, objects, and people—to show portraits of the greatest of all subjects—his beloved Son. This book examines eight such Old Testament pictures and demonstrates how they point us forward to Jesus Christ, the coming King.

'This book is an excellent evangelistic tool, particularly because it allows the eyes of our understanding to see Jesus through a number of "pictures" in the Old Testament. Whereas the Western world majors in abstract thought, I expect this book to find special appeal with us here in Africa where picture language is the way of communication. This book should be put into the hands of those who need to hear the gospel afresh in this simple picture form. I cannot commend it too highly!'
CONRAD MBEWE, PASTOR OF KABWATA BAPTIST CHURCH, LUSAKA, ZAMBIA

'Kurt Strassner's *Hints and Signs of the Coming King* provides an attractive guidebook to help us discover for ourselves how the Old Testament points to Jesus. What's more, you can read it, enjoy it, and learn life-long principles for your own Bible study—all in about the same length of time as a walk from Jerusalem to Emmaus. Enjoy the journey!'
SINCLAIR B FERGUSON, SENIOR MINISTER, FIRST PRESBYTERIAN CHURCH, COLUMBIA, SOUTH CAROLINA

Pathways to peace

Facing the future with faith—
Meditations from Isaiah 40

JOHN KITCHEN

128PP, PAPERBACK

ISBN 978-1-84625-212-9

A million events assault the word tomorrow to make it the most uncertain word in the English language. As we stand at the threshold between a fretful past and a wishful future, what guarantee is there that tomorrow will be better than yesterday? Pathways to Peace sets forth the hope of Isaiah 40: Only God's presence sustains you in the panic of an uncertain future, and God's presence only helps you when you appreciate his preeminence over all things. Where God is lifted up as preeminent, he manifests his presence and the peace of God is the result in the believer's life..

'John Kitchen's book on Isaiah 40 is a joy to read with its strong encouragement on how the preeminence and presence of our Lord affects all we do, think, and hope for as believers. I strongly encourage a wide usage of this book among all who need a spiritual uplift in these troubling days.'
WALTER C. KAISER, JR., PRESIDENT EMERITUS, GORDON-CONWELL THEOLOGICAL SEMINARY

'This is a refreshing and health-giving meditation on the grandest of all themes: the nature of God and how it affects our living today. It will strengthen your spiritual muscles and equip you to face the challenges you encounter victoriously.'
AJITH FERNANDO, NATIONAL DIRECTOR, YOUTH FOR CHRIST, SRI LANKA

On wings of prayer
Praying the ACTS way

REGGIE WEEMS

112PP, PAPERBACK

ISBN 978-1-84625-178-8

Constructing a prayer life is often like putting a puzzle together without the box's cover. Having a picture makes all the difference. Bible prayers create a model of what prayer can be; exciting, fulfilling and powerful. Using a simple acrostic makes prayer memorable, interesting and focused. You too can learn to pray following this simple outline utilized by men and women who experience the transforming power of prayer.

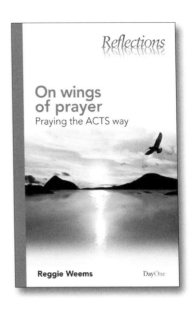

'This brief work on prayer will encourage you to pray, teach you to pray, and give you precious gems about prayer along the way. It taught me things I did not know, and reminded me of things I had forgotten.'
PAUL DAVID WASHER, HEARTCRY MISSIONARY SOCIETY

'Because of the unique nature of the Christian discipline of prayer, most books on prayer are more inspiring than they are helpful. Pastor Reggie Weems has achieved what only a few have ever done in Christian history. This book is orthodox, penetrating, motivating and inspiring, all in one slender, readable volume. If you are hoping to enhance your walk with the Master, here is one book that will bless your soul.'
PAIGE PATTERSON, PRESIDENT, SOUTHWESTERN BAPTIST THEOLOGICAL SEMINARY, FORT WORTH, TEXAS, USA

Under God's smile
The Trinitarian Blessing of
2 Corinthians 13:14

DEREK PRIME

128PP, PAPERBACK

ISBN 978-1-84625-059-0

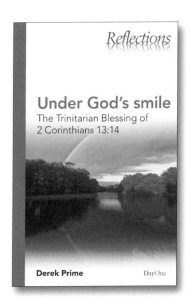

During recent decades, it has become the practice of Christians in many churches and in university and college Christian Unions to commit one another to God's grace and care with the words 'May the grace of the Lord Jesus Christ, and the love of God, and the fellowship of the Holy Spirit be with us all' (2 Corinthians 13:14). They are familiar words, but what do they actually mean? For what are we praying?

So that we do not repeat these words without appreciating their full implication, Derek Prime explores them and considers the three Persons of the Trinity in their different, yet perfectly harmonious, relationship to every believer. Written in an easy-to-read style, this book is thoroughly rooted in the Scriptures and is a demonstration that solid biblical truth is both heart-warming and exciting.

'Wholesome food for the average Christian reader and devotional writing of the highest order'
EVANGELICALS NOW

'An easily-read book, helpful in all stages of Christian life'
GRACE MAGAZINE

'Derek Prime's ministry is much appreciated by many Christian groups, including ourselves. Like all his other books … biblically based and easy to read'
ASSOCIATED PRESBYTERIANS NEWS

'If, like me, you are constantly on the lookout for books that say a great deal in short order, you will be delighted by what you hold in your hand. It is a special gift not only to expound what the blessing of the triune God means, but also to explain why it matters. We have come to expect this from Derek Prime, and once again he hits the mark.'
ALISTAIR BEGG, SENIOR PASTOR, PARKSIDE CHURCH, CHAGRIN FALLS, OHIO